Tulips for Elsie

Tulips for Elsie

Poems by Jonathan Potter

KORREKTIV PRESS

Seattle ✱ New Orleans ✱ Copenhagen

For permissions and ordering information, visit:
www.korrektivpress.com

First Edition

ISBN: 978-0-9831513-0-2

Library of Congress Control Number: 2021935866

And for HP & DP

Who sing me tulip songs both day and night

☉　☽　○　☾

My eldest daughter's moon reflects my sun.
My youngest daughter's sun collects my moon.
The woven strands of stars undone
Within my mind begin to weave a tune
That sings around me in a tunic form
With threads of gravity and mystery
To shield my field against the wind and warm
The wintry past with future history.

♒　♐　♊　♓

And for NW

The only begetter of the ensuing

Tulips of my mind

I'll be your Lone Ranger
If you'll be my Tonto
In Montreal
If not in Toronto

Contents

Prologue

On Becoming a Godmother

by Helen Campbell

On the occasion of the birth of Elsie Reifenberger
    25 January 1912

Deep in white winter the child was born.
It had been snowing day and night and then
With eighteen inches on the ground it quit.
No wind, no glaze of ice, just powdered snow
To sink down in at every long, long step.
Now every month the pastor of this place
Went to the city for communion wine, and
Out of a long ennui behind his stove,
Doing my Cicero and trying to think
Quod Erat Demonstrandum I made plans
To ride out to the farm with a potted flower,
To have the pastor buy a hyacinth,
Send for a flower for the flower loving,
The mother of the child.
                              I got permission
To ride the pastor's mare out to the farm.
Kate was a mare one mounted *au galop*,
A flying leap and then, bit in the teeth,
Hell bent for parts unknown, she ran a mile
Before she slowed and became an excellent mount.
All thought the snow would cramp her style this time,
That I could carry a potted hyacinth,
A white hyacinth breathing a fog of smell
In my right arm.

From the water trough I sprang!
Off to the races! All is well, I thought.
Down hill and up she ran. Then going through town
There was a wooden crossing under the snow.
Snow partly melted made it slippery.
Kate fell on her side, the potted hyacinth
Out of its pot, but neatly, in the snow.

I spilled the other way, my left instep
Under the saddle horn. The mare got up
Trembling, wild-eyed and trembling. I held on
To reins and while she stood scooped up the flower,
Its stem unbroken, put it back in the pot,
And got back on. More or less at a walk
Kate waded through the snow out to the farm.

In a warm room, under beautiful eyes
I held the new-born child
A smallish girl, looking old and wise
Yet brand new and mild.

We did not talk, listened to snow,
Knew pain, hyacinth breath,
Fire in the stove and lamplight glow,
Generations of death.

Women pass motherhood to girls
Letting them hold their young.
An eon of feeling thus unfurls
From the small thing among

Its new soft wrappings. All forgiving
Generations of life
Swoop in the blood. This part of living
Makes a girl almost a wife.

It had been snowing day and night. The drifts
Smoothed over fences, banked the walls but good.
In every stovepipe fire roared. Sweet flame
Took fine wood and pitch logs. Warmth of cattle
And horses rose in the barn. Kate ate her ration
Of oats and hay and carrots, wild eyes closed.
A rub-down and the blanket off! Bundle
Of legs and snorts, Kate, menacing rump
That slammed the unwary saddler against the stall.
Now the perdition out of her, she munched
Carrots, eyes closed, but ears up listening
While she was told the hellishness of her ways.

That day, that night, white hyacinths, the mare,
The cold, the fire vanishing in time
Made me god-mother to a babe that smiled.

Q. E. D.

Tulips for Elsie

The day before you died I thought I'd bring
You tulips for your bedside table, bright
Ones, pink and white, to give your gaze a place
To rest, to make your labor seem less harsh.
I told my daughter so, my four-year-old
Who'd told me I should visit you, who'd hinted:
Your work, this dying business you were in,
Was making worldly things seem flimsy, thin.
The day moved on and tulips left my mind, though,
Until I thought of you again, too late,
The night descending, bringing sleep's regrets.
The morning came and with its obligations
Distracting me, I let my dream of tulip
Fields plow under and turned to hear the news.

The River

I need the river,
the way it carries the
spring runoff in its arms
like a mother,
the way it glides like
a roller blader, like
bearings in fresh oil,
like a drunken thought
in the mind of a happy man.
I need the river
like that man needs that drink
at the end of a long day.
The river bends and blends
in eddies and backwaters,
slackwaters and rapids and glints,
nudges and fingers and fists,
velvety nuzzles at sunset.

In the shallows here, midstream,
a moose looks over
with drizzling muzzle
and chewing cud,
not a cartoon moose,
but a shimmering hulk
of bone and hide and antler,
tendon and flesh and pulsing veins.
So I carry myself on downstream
and listen for
crawdad-scuttle, tail-slap,
frog-swish, fish-flutter,
the swirls and swansongs,
the killdeer and swallow
that inhabit my waking dreams,
the hinting whispers
that speak at dawn.

I need the river ghosts
and the river spirits
to whisper their secrets
in my ears, to tell me
the news from upstream,
to silence the demons in my head,
to show me the light that
dances on the riverbed.
The river makes of its rocks
a mosaic unfurling,
not an abstract but a concrete
pattern that paints
music on my eyes,
and sings my pain: away.
I need my pain and I
need the river
to sing it away.

I need the power of the river
to flow through my soul,
to turn the turbines of my mind.
I need to feel it and smell it
and see it and hear it.
I need to taste and see,
taste and see, kneeling,
my reflection, darkly.
I need the river
to carry my burdens,
not like a mule or an ox
or a train or a truck
but like an angel descending,
like an easement from on high,
the power and the glory
flowing to the sea
where we all are destined to be.

River, I call to thee.
Make me one of your people, let me
follow you down,
let me follow you downstream.

Wounded by Light

If I say to you the cage of my heart is
bent and bleeding birds into the sky,
a moth is dazzled by the blinding sky,
an airplane tears the silence of the sky,
you may empty my words like pebbles
from your shoes and walk away.
Squint at the horizon through a smudged window —
there are moments to exchange for days, for years.
Close your eyes and open doors
and falling in the rain will come my name.

If someone asks you if you have seen
the something she lost, you could say
you could make a wish through the window.
There are instruments and experiments
and many words for many things —
a moth dusting her wings on a windowpane,
a bird on a wire, a man on a telephone
listening for a voice to speak his name.
There is a stepping aside, a turning around,
a name withheld like a caged bird.

At the end of the day the sun is in my boots
and I walk across a dismal craving.
The sky is a seamless puzzle I cannot solve
and it hurts my mind to try to.
In mirrors made of windows your image grieves.
You drop your name like a stone,
a sparrow falling, a moth wounded by light.

Seventy Syllables for My Mother

The birds of paradise are flying past
The windows of the room where you were born.
The agents of intelligence are laid
To rest where documents were blackened out;
Their ghosts, deleted, cannot harm your dreams,
Your dreams interrogated by your life,
Your dreams like grapes crushed in the winepress
And transubstantiated to Christ's blood.
The swallows and the sparrows of late autumn
Return to where they came from in the spring;
They drink the sunset water from the pool
And follow something written in the bones
Which time cannot recall but faith foretells,
Which fear blots out but love in blood respells.

November 22, 1989

The day I met Walker, the rain had fallen
in Louisiana sheets, and I'd left
my tent illicitly pitched in the Bogue Falaya
State Park, along with a bookish bottle
of Early Times I'd taken a few swigs off of
in the dark the night before as pinecones pitched
and fell outside as if in triadic morse code
from Flannery in heaven telling me grace was in
the river. And alligators, too, I reckoned.
I walked the cracked sidewalks of Covington, aimlessly,
dazed by the wonder of seeing vines sprouting
through the cracks in a sacramental vision,
a concelebration of namer and named,
and leapt across the flashflood puddles
as I made my way towards no destination
but found myself in The Kumquat bookstore
to ogle shelves bursting with signed copies of
The Moviegoer, *The Last Gentleman*, *Love in the Ruins*,
Lancelot, *The Second Coming*, *The Thanatos Syndrome*,
Lost in the Cosmos, *The Message in the Bottle*, books
that had changed my life. Oh Walker (Oh Rory)
I was twenty-four and pining for a woman
From whom I was also on the run in triangular
despair (yet thanks in part to you I also
was aware—at least a little—a foothold—
of the despair, contrary to that Kierkegaardian
epigraph, precisely pitched though it is).
Oh Walker: so I bought a stack of books,
some for me and some for those I loved,
and left instructions with the keeper of
the store to have you encode, in your
physician's scrawl, your cracked prescriptions
where the vines of love and truth might grow
from bourbon and ink, the cumulative bliss of limitation,
where you and I might clear a space for being.

When I Was Broke

When I was broke and money spent
I pawned my board to pay the rent;
To buy some beer to ease my ache
I sold my car for pity's sake
And walked to where the road was bent.

When darkness hit and made a dent
Against whatever light had meant,
I laid down hearts and let them break
When I was broke.

When I awoke not to repent,
The sunlight seemed not heaven sent
But blinking in I let it make
My heart lick frosting from the cake
That someone left outside my tent
When I was broke.

After Sonnet 128

How often you, my secret music, play
Across the cells I live in in my brain,
Two thousand million miles and more away
From your piano—kilometers of pain.
It's true I see and hear you through the screen,
And possible I may compel you to sing,
To show the tender inward of your being
(With touches to your conscience and your ring).
But envy has no place in this affair.
The keys of your piano do not kiss
Your hand the way we kissed in the open air
Of that strange night of drunk, truncated bliss.
But fingers, lips, they make no difference now;
They only want what miles will not allow.

After I Want You

I hear the angels' silver saxophones
Announcing the savior's birth in Bethlehem
And telling me I should recall my bones
And how they're destined to be dust and grime.
Should I refuse the enticements of the time
We met and found ourselves falling under
A spell we willed upon each other, madam?
I wasn't born in Bethlehem, far from it.
I'm more like old Adam, born in a paradise
Soon lost. But found again, perhaps, in
Your loveliness, forbidden, bidden, sin.
How to proceed then, drinking from this cup,
Yes, broken, sipping of the blood of him
Who glances down on us with mercy grim?

Gray Whale

gray whale skeleton
glued together and mounted
near the ocean shore

After Take This Waltz

Oh Kemosabe, the river's disguise has fallen
Off, the masked man has lost his horse
And now is crawling through the desert of
His ego, pride, and unrequited love songs,
His catalog of lies, his almanac of wrongs,
His lifelong habit of missing the boat, his time
And anger management issues, his secret waltz,
His narcissistic heigh-ho silver flourish,
His impatience for adventure's broken arch,
His buttoned shirts containing too much starch,
Oh Kemosabe, love, my love, my love,
The scrapbook shut, my eyes wide open, you
The waltz I long to dance, the flood I long
To swim, the sky I want to sing this song.

Prepositions

If you can fall on me and I on you
And under you and in you
In hotel rooms and AirBnBs,
Perhaps that will appease
The weakness in our knees
And help us make it through
Our other miseries.

Good Night

So here we are and here we aren't, neither
Here nor there, you not in my arms,
My body not in yours, both of us clinging
To a far off night and the memory of a dream,
Both of us struggling with the frayed edges of the night,
This night and the hundred nights that lie
Before us and the four-score more,
The fabric unraveling against the closed door
Between us, the continental divide, the wind
That carries my thoughts to you and carries yours
Back to me in the night on streams of dreams,
Good night, love, good night, this is my
Good night to you and yours to me, good night,
Good night, good night, good night, good night, good night.

Audubon's Lament

The bird that breathed beneath my brush
Is dead.
The beak beyond the paint on paper
Cried
Out silence in my dream this morning
When the sun
Crept in my bedroom window
With the turning Earth's orbit's
Arc.
I woke to wake and put my day
Down —
And have not risen since.
The wings of morning wept,
The sparrows in the bush
Did hush.

The Buzzards

The buzzards are perched on my limbs
My cousins converge on the scene
The blind elephant from my dream
Begins to trumpet madly and sadly
A little girl I once knew
Climbs onto a westbound train in a distant city
No longer is she a little girl but a young woman
With plans and dreams unfolding
The sky is blue but a fog settles in
The streets are empty
The fog thickens and I can no longer see
My hands reaching out in front of me

The Endless Moment

Some blue sky has appeared
out my office window.
My thoughts are there,
eastward towards Montreal,
climbing the clouds, grasping
at air, constructing wishes
out of patches of old sunlight,
and painting your picture with
the brushes of ancient memory
refashioned in love
for the endless moment
I want to spend with you now.

I Want You

I want to run my fingers through the flames
Of your fiery hair, feel the fabric of
Your love, the weave of your life in my calloused hands,
I want to feel you up close, pressed
Against me for a long moment that lingers
For days, I want all of you and parts
Of you, I want to collect you and keep you
If only for that moment. And if I may
I want to find my way inside you to
The very depths of you, to learn every contour
And fold of you, and then simply to be
With you, entirely, without fear, without
The past, without the future, only now
And only you and me and fire and light

The Airport

When you arrived I saw you from a long
Way off. I stood there smiling. This would be
Our first kiss since Baltimore, the first
Collision of our bodies since that oddly
Unfettered night that ended with our clothing
Not falling together to the floor in your
Room or mine, but rather just a kiss
Goodnight, no further. But now I'd be remiss
To stop at that and you would, too, because,
Well now, my fingers in the fire of
Your hair, our lips, our skin—all of it—
Alive, aflutter, our bodies having waited,
Our minds and souls having co-authored every word
Of a beautiful book of longing, we now go further.

Driving Down Division

Annie wants a baby now
Annie wants a baby any way she can
   — Red Hot Chili Peppers

Prologue

Division Street divides Spokane like a scar
from stem to stern
from north to south
dividing west from east
heart from liver
on one side you
will find Al's Motel
with hourly rates
and permanently stained sheets
and on the other side St. Al's church
its Ignatian plates
and desolate consolations
in the middle you will
find yourself in transit
driving down Division.

The Past

I wake up tied up
to a bed in Al's Motel
the taste of sawdust in my mouth
what time is it? the April sky
is overcast overeasy
pigeon shit on the window
stains my view
and I strain at the thought of
how did that pigeon shit
fly sideways to land there?

there's a song in my head
Annie wants a baby
she was my love long ago
many missing pieces ago
before the millionth abortion
before I left and lost my head
the room is surprisingly clean
it reeks of cigarettes and stale perfume
but the reek is a grace note
threading through the death march
playing a throbbing in my brain
the reek is a puzzle piece
that might fit somewhere
if I could only find the puzzle
if I could only untie these knots
bitch, that bitch tied me up
and took my money
by the looks of it
she even took my boots
and the sunlight I saved inside those boots
that bitch but who could blame her.

The Future

I fall asleep kneeling at the altar rail
in St. Al's church, Christ like a
piece of a puzzle on my tongue
tasting like sawdust but washed down
with wine and blood, accident and substance
the stained-glass windows black in the dark
my soul black but washed clean
ready to burn white
now and at the time of my death
O brother death, O bright wings
over the bent world
over my bent soul

over the gaping hole in my bent soul
the gaping godshaped hole
there's a song in my head
Annie wants a baby
she was my love long ago
and now I see her dark eyes
the church is cluttered with statues
and cast-off sins swept by the wind
like puzzle pieces scattered
the leftover smell of incense and oil
a hospital for sinners
or a morgue
it makes no difference to my soul
ascending
it makes no difference to my spirit
flying
I don't look back
my hand is on the plow
my boots are far below
the moon setting the sun rising
blameless, eternal, alive.

The Present

You Can Call Me Al
is playing on the radio
I'm driving down Division
and I am divided
you can call me Al
or you can call me Zimmy
you can call me Simon
or you can call me Garfunkel
I am a man divided
and there's a crack in my windshield
it runs the length of it
there's a crack in my soul

and ice that wants to wedge there
to break me in two
something wants to split me
and destroy me
but something else
with fiery wings
wants to drive down in me
down my division
and weld me together
I can see that now
I can see a bird high overhead
it might be an eagle or a big hawk, hunting
swooping and diving
I keep driving
through the sweet smell of my own sweat
down Division down into the city
my boot sole gentle on the gas pedal
down town down
into the heart of it
a new song comes on
Annie wants a baby
missing pieces she's got
a lot of them
so do I, so do I.

Spokane Stanzas

Spokane's the place where water falling
From Idaho runs through with thoughts
Unconsciously unwinding, reeling
The poets in from inland squats
To take their places at the river's
Bedraggled edges. Poets' livers
Can't filter all that they abuse
Themselves with for the lovely ruse
That lines of words can make unhappy
Inhabitants of Coeur d'Alene
Cease for a moment feeling pain
Or leastwise help them feel less crappy
When turning towards the Cascade heights
With thoughts of oceanic nights.

Tom I. Davis

Tom Davis, inauspicious, rivered
In Peaceful Valley, didn't miss
The point, the little jests delivered
From points upstream, the hugs and piss
Of landscapes peopled through all seasons
With love and love's subtle treasons,
The unforlorn beatitudes
Of losses, pains, of thoughts and moods,
The here and now's eclipse diminished
By wives and children, poems, lies,
And truth writ small within the lines
Until that gnarled finger finished
His last touch, his last salute
To life, though silent, never mute.

Dennis Held

He polkas two step flops out of the
Serene dead ends of Vinegar Flats
Where time and time's children love the
Unhurried pace. The sidestreet cats
Meander round the poet's broken
Heart, beat up car, aching
Iambic lines laid out like seeds
In rows where syllables and weeds
Comingle with pugnacious music
In step with river rush and trains
That sing to Dennis soft refrains
And bathe the tragic in the comic
Insistence on the rocky ground
Divine in dialects of sound.

Zan Agzigian

A flame from Sandra, both eyes open—
A tape-recorded organ drones,
A spirit forces them for pardon
So full of tears and telephones.
In insulated Spokane houses
October Spokane windy punches
Handled our hearts with sleight of hand
In absolute pastures of chambered grassland.
Zan caught the truth and sent it flying
Inside our music, note for note
To help survive the springtime bite
Of being born while busy dying.
No fooling Zan's become this place,
There is a God, she found the trace.

Jonathan Johnson

J. Johnson came to Spokane's urban
Environs tracking mud across
The academic carpet, carbon
Dating mastodons of loss
Put up for sale in Fairbanks' paper,
Domestic, edgeless, Great Lakes clipper
Delivering Jonathan to our town,
A mountain man in poet's gown,
Intense, awake, a patient teacher,
A husband, father, one who knows
The shape of silence and what grows
From silence into human nature.
Dear Jon, the jar you placed in Cheney
Filled up with Burns Night's blossom's honey.

Christopher Howell

He rose up from a farm near Portland
And ranged a Lutheran college north;
Seattle beaconed down, and heartland
Unmindfulness propelled him forth
Beyond a war of naval typists,
Their visions rival solipsists
Undoing; lately in the man
Arriving here to make Spokane
The house of his body, snowing lightly,
A lucky crime, the crime of luck,
But mercy holds his hand; he's stuck
For now but angels come fortnightly
To sing him over heaven's bridge
From jagged ridge to jagged ridge.

Rachel Toor

The watch that rests near angels dancing
Upon —around —your nimble wrist
Tells more than time at every glancing
When even demons giving blist-
Ers notice your released endorphins
Undoing pain, unnailing coffins,
And resurrecting running shoes
For one more run in search of clues
To what makes Academe's demented
Professors tic, what makes us fall
Into profound abstracted fol-
Ly: tenure tracks down halls cemented
With chalky dreams and clocks that click
Their heels to run on time, and quick.

Jess Walter

Your name recalls that farfetched Jesse—
The outlaw James whose name came down
The falls and tumbled graves of history,
Like Springdale dogs the floods won't drown.
Your books pile up, basalt-like columns
Beneath them, reporters' stratagems
From ink to paper, one eye dark
But one enough to light a spark.
Evince the witness of the breaking
Unbroken ground of needless naught
Within your grasp but dearly bought—
Self-loathing but not self-forsaking.
Your soul, dear Jess, is nonetheless
The ruins that I'd have God bless.

Sherman Alexie

The Spokane falls where ghosts of salmon
Foreseen by Sherman fill their gills
With Catholic gilt and white man's mammon
To pay for rehabs and oil pills,
Basalt and concrete worn by water
Flowing genocidal slaughter,
Coyote's unrequited love,
Alexie's push that comes to shove.
The towns of Wellpinit and Reardan,
The left and right arms that draw
You to Spokane's hungry maw,
Release you now; but do not harden
The paths of your own tears that trail
Down windows in Seattle's vale.

Kurt Olson

    grew up in Clarkston, but the river
And falls, the whispers and glances, the side-
Walk life, the upright's strings aquiver
Beneath his touch, made him decide
To chance it north, to break his language
In two or three, to speak the garbage
Out, out, to dumpster dive
His soul and come back out alive
With music that was lost on fathers
(Ungiven, unforgiven, lost)
And words beneath forgotten crust
Cast out in alleys where no one bothers
With berries from Kurt's favorite pie,
The filling filling up his sky.

Mark Anderson

My cousin Mark, his mouth a jumble
Of broken word and spoken mic
Syllabic gleams between his humble
Chaotic teeth, his Eastern psych
Degree a background velvet curtain
In mind unwound, laid out, uncertain
Of what the world is asking of
The god no one believes in, love,
And love's irascible homely cousin,
Lust, whose arrows break like lead
In pencils pressed against one's head
But fly like roses by the dozen
Into the hearts of Spokane's youth
To bloom in light and bomb in truth.

Thom Caraway

The Spokane flows the right direction
Away from North Dakota, with
The Empire Builder gaining traction
Towards the coast and mountain's wrath.
Inside the train, a car away from
Dakota's oceanic daydream,
Thom dines on salmon steak filet,
Adjusts his laurel-wreathed beret,
And watches good ideas grow better
As small-town architects increase
Their sense of timing, form, and grace,
As morning comes and thoughts grow lighter.
Then Thom wakes in his Spokane bed
Where train dreams end with daily bread.

Spokane

The grit and the gristle
The sweat and the muscle

The grinding wheels
The aching whistle

Of the train
Going through downtown

What Catches Also Grabs

what catches my eye
(pileated woodpecker)
also grabs my ear

Short Story

I. The Boxer Rebellion

Your turn of that page
has opened a drawer.
My home. I am his underwear.

He'll always show you
the contents of his drawers
but never what he's wearing.

He's that kind of fellow.
But I'll give you a clue:
I am his only pair of boxers.

To put it briefly,
he suffers a shortage.
Why only one of me?

Why only one day
of freedom per week
when he could have seven?

That is the question
I once heard
his girlfriend ask.

He replied like Robert Frost
that a little freedom
is almost too much

and went home and
put on briefs.
Short changed.

II. A Brief History of the Work Week

Brief #1 (Sunday)
Freedom's just another word for lost
In funhouse laundromats where dreams are tossed.

Brief #2 (Monday)
You've got to work to make a living wage,
You've got to button up your daily rage.

Brief #3 (Tuesday)
You've got to count your syllables and keep
Your cock and scrotum snug and fast asleep.

Brief #4 (Wednesday)
You've got to keep your humpday hopes pressed down,
It makes no difference if you smile or frown.

Brief #5 (Thursday)
You might love her, she might love you, but then
Your Adam's apple bulges up again.

Brief #6 (Friday)
Thank God? Well, maybe in the morning light,
But Eden's underwear gets torn at night.

Brief Chorus (all together)
Like Frost said, don't play tennis without net.
Don't let your balls fly free from match to set.

III. The Girl Who Was Saturday

I like it when my man is frisky
But when he drinks too much
He gets so frisky
Like a shooting star on a Saturday night
He shines so bright but then he passes out.

I like it when he takes me out dancing,
I like it when he cuts loose a little bit, you know,
On a Saturday night after a long week of work,
When he takes off that tie and loosens up his collar.

I like it when my man gets frisky
And I like to drink and have a good time
But if he drinks too much too fast
He passes out too soon
And when I'm ready
For the fun to continue on, he's gone.

He's lying there in his boxer shorts.
I love those boxers,
The ones with the palm trees
And the Christmas lights,
He looks so peaceful sleeping there,
Like an angel, like a soldier, like a child,
But I want my man to wake up and take me
To the promised land.

I like it when my man is frisky,
When he's had just a little whisky.
But when I see him on a Wednesday or a Thursday,
He never has those boxers on,
He's wound up tight and white,
But I love my man when he gets frisky
On a Saturday night.

IV. The Naked Poet Speaks

O boxers, I hear the siren call
Of your easy-open fly
And your free and airy ways.

O briefs, you've
Held me close and kept me
Safe since childhood.

O Adam, O Eve, O Fruit
Of the loom, what have you wrought?
Who told you you were naked?

Since childhood, I've been
Burdened and blessed with the words
For the days of the week.

I've been clothed
With the fabric of toil and dread,
Of yesterday and tomorrow.

But now I stand undressed
Before the dresser of my shame,
I stare into the abyss of my drawers.

In this present moment
I ask of you, O Robert Frost: speak
Your will and testament to me.

V. The Shorts Not Worn
With apologies to Robert Frost and his underwear

Two shorts submerged in a yellow drawer
And sorry I could not model both
And be one wearer, long I wore
The tighter briefs till I was sore
And then I bent and scratched my undergrowth.

Then took the boxers, just as fair
And having no doubt the looser fit
They were the ones I wanted to wear;
So easy to whip it out and piss anywhere,
The opening truly being made for it.

And both that morning equally lay
In my drawer with shirtsers and socksers.
Oh, I kept the briefs for another day!
Yet knowing how freedom has to have its way
I doubted if I should ever change from boxers.

I shall be telling this with a sigh
In the Bartlett ages and ages hence.
Two pairs of shorts in a drawer, and I —
I wore the ones more loose to thigh
And that has made all the difference.

Stopping by Blogs on a Frosty Evening

Whose blog this is, a neo-con,
His book is available on Amazon.
He will not see me lurking here;
My comments all will be anon.

My online friends won't think it queer
If I blog while drinking a six-pack of beer
Between dinner and the ten o'clock news;
It fills my comments with good cheer.

My wife has the spouse-of-a-blogger blues
And asks me if I've noticed her cues.
The only other sound's the click
Of mouse and key as I peruse

This blog and the next one till I'm sick
Of beating a dead horse with a stick
And another evening's burned its wick,
And another evening's burned its wick.

The Condom

An act of hope — I'd overcome
my teenage embarrassment
and dread at the Five and Dime
to buy a pack of Trojans,
and stuck one in my pocket that night,
that Friday night when, despite
there being not a girl in sight,
I'd hoped, as young men do, I might
get lucky after the football game,
or at halftime even, and win
the lose-your-virginity lottery —
and here was my ticket.

The condom, pristine, unused,
still rested there snug as a
bug in a rug (or as a well-protected
quarterback with nobody open)
when my mom came through
gathering laundry for her
Saturday wash. I watched her hand
reach in and penetrate
the inner sanctum of that pocket,
seeking things to save from
the violence of the wash cycle.

And then it hit me what she'd found.
I lunged like a linebacker
across the small cluttered
space of my bedroom and snatched
the condom from her washer woman grip.
What was that? she said.
Oh nothing, came my reply. Wait,
you really don't know?
No, I have no idea, she lied.
She lied and I was grateful
for that lie. But still regretful
that I'd not got laid.

The Night Before the First Day of School

With Apologies to St. Nick

'Twas the first day of school, when all through the class
Not a brain cell was stirring and I needed a pass;
My classmates were sitting like lumps in their chairs,
Hoping the teacher would fall down the stairs.
The principal hid in her office and cried
While the flowers of summer wilted and died;
And mamma with her suntan and dad with his beer
Had just waved goodbye and got the hell outta here,
When out on the playground there arose such a clatter,
I sprang from my desk to see what was the matter.
Away to the window I flew like a flash,
Tore open the shutters and threw up the sash.
The teacher freaked out and said, Sit back down!
We don't need such behavior from a would-be class clown!
When what to my wondering eyes did appear
But a gigantic monster truck that was hitting third gear,
With a little old driver so lively and quick,
I knew in a moment he was a lunatic.
More rapid than seagulls his curses they came,
And he whistled, and squawked, and called out my name.
Oh shit, I thought, this lunatic's fixin'
To demolish the school like a linebacker blitzin'.
I said to my classmates, We can't wait for the bell,
Now dash away! dash away! Like bats outta hell.
As leaves that before the wild hurricane fly,
When they meet with an obstacle, mount to the sky;
So out of the schoolhouse everyone flew
With backpacks full of books (and some with weed too).
And then, in a twinkling, I heard on the street
The flipping and flapping of flip-flop-clad feet.
As I leapt from the schoolyard and was turning around,
The dude in the truck made a cackling sound.
He put on the brakes and skidded to a stop;

I'm not really a lunatic, he said, I'm a cop
And I'm here to arrest you for grade school truancy
And make you learn math and linguistic fluency.
His eyes—how they twinkled! his dimples, how scary!
His cheeks were like roses, his nose like a cherry!
His droll little mouth was drawn up in a frown
And the beard on his chin was dirt-like and brown.
The stump of an e-cig he held tight in his teeth,
And the vapor encircled his head like a wreath;
He had a broad face and a little round belly
That shook when he laughed, like a bowl full of jelly.
He was chubby and plump like a horror movie elf,
And I screamed when I saw him and wet myself;
A wink of his eye and a twist of his head
Confirmed that I had something to dread;
He spoke not a word, but went straight to his work,
Rounding us up and being a jerk.
Then poking his finger deep into his nose,
He said, You've been binge watching too many shows.
But then all of a sudden I heard a loud whistle
That tore at my brain like a thorn on a thistle.
It was my mom waking me up and turning on the light—
"Happy first day of school, did you sleep well last night?"

Wine Glasses

wine glasses are hard
not to break when you throw them
from a speeding car

Happy Birthday Dear Pushkin

From Seattle in 1889

On Pushkin's birthday, Eighteen-Eighty-
Nine (ninety years old the bard
Would be, but for romantic fate he
Gave up his life, a cast-off shard
Cast off too soon), Seattle kindled
From gluey scrap where sharpies swindled
The downtown down-and-outers out
Of weekly pay for Skid Road clout
With seamstress' skirts and garters seeming
Undone for doing what we do
When left to our devices, through
The rise and fall, the devil's steaming
Pile of what you will, a choir
Of angels singing round the fire.

John Back

"When I throw the water on, the glue flew all over the shop into the shavings and everything take fire." ... shortly after ... John Back left Seattle.

John Back, a Swede with lanky beard,
Was heating glue and feeling sick.
The glue smell always made a weird
Sensation in his throat, like thick
Molasses spread on char-burned toast
Each time he took a breath or swallowed.
John turned his back and thought a ghost
Said something in his ear. What followed
Made John wheel back around to see
The glue, now hot and getting hotter,
Was boiling over — blazingly —
Which made John grab a pail of water.
The water spread the gluey flame
And John left town and changed his name.

Rat Town Burns

… no one got hurt in the fire, but it was reported that one million rats were consumed in the flames.

They say a million rats laid down
Their lives the day Seattle blazed
To ash. The town within the town
Asleep: nocturnal rats unfazed
By daytime noises gone awry—
Such dreams of fish and apple pie
In ovens, crusts and marmalades
In garbage cans for midnight raids
Danced through, from cell to cell, their small
Uncluttered rodent brains as flame
Consumed with wagging tongue the lame
And fat ones first but nearly all
In crackling bites. The lithe ones woke
But only soon enough to choke.

Saloon Closed

Mayor Moran declared an 8:00 p.m. curfew that night
and ordered all remaining saloons closed until further notice.

The mayor in his wisdom, turning
From flames outside his window's view,
Declared that—with this fire burning
The whole damn town by nail and screw—
The citizens should not be drinking
From wells of fire water (thinking
That booze might ease the pain of ash
Or make a fire line of cash
For workman's wages turned to embers);
No, better call the night a day,
Let ashes cool and dreams be gay:
Of wet Novembers and Decembers
And sitting by the fireside,
Hot buttered rum, and Christmastide.

Wiped Out

*"... a horrible black smudge, as though a Hand had come down
and rubbed the place smooth. I know now what being wiped out means."*

The ruddy Kipling in a boat
Was touring Puget Sound the day
Seattle burned. He wrote a note
About the sight of soot that lay
Across the landscape like a smudge
Some Hand (divine? infernal?) left
Where once a city stood. The grudge
That Being held—to leave bereft
A town, wiped out, crossed out, erased—
Raised questions of the shape of Love;
And yet no souls were lost, the waste
A miracle uncertain of
Interpretation till the light
That failed became reborn in sight.

Sebastian Ness

One man found a large lump of melted gold and the haste with which he shoved it under his coat and made off was astonishing. He was chased several blocks by the police, but was not captured.

Sebastian Ness was kicking through the
Still cooling ash at First and Main
When something solid led him to the
Enticing thought that not in vain
A gloved hand might venture, bending,
To touch some mystery, depending
On fortune's smile to turn his fate
From lead to gold, to love from hate.
The lump he lifted flamed like foil
Beneath the blue, bird-speckled skies,
And Ness took flight with silent cries
That oozed out from his soul like oil.
His feet were fleet and did not pause
To ponder morals, rights, or laws.

Adam Connel

A couple of alert young guardsmen apprehended a man clothed in four new suits.

A man named Adam Connel, lurking
Behind the shell of what had been
The tailor's—where his wife was working
When fire'd come like Adam's sin—
Peeked in. Against the soot, red dapples
Attracted his attention: apples
His wife had left behind, unburned
Somehow and sweet, so Adam turned
And, seeing no one looking, hastened
Within to have a taste. The juice
Was dribbling down his chin like sluice
When Adam saw the suits. They glistened
Like royal robes of silken thread.
So Adam put them on and fled.

Kipling Haunted by the Ghost of Pushkin

"No one, not even the Government, knows the number of islands in the Sound. Even now you can get one almost for the asking; can build a house, raise sheep, catch salmon, and become a king on a small scale." —R.K.

When Kipling left Seattle's ashes
Behind and navigated north
Toward Vancouver, gentle splashes
At prow and rocking back and forth
With island views at every turning,
The ghost of Pushkin, spirit yearning
To flow again in blood and ink,
Appeared to him and bade him think
About the island kingdom every
Moran or Murphy might create
From fire of love and ash of hate
Away from worldly woe and thievery—
But only to flame up like hay
When lightning strikes on Judgment Day.

The Legend of John Back's Death

As legend has it, whether true or
Perhaps a tallish tale, John Back
Was dry and needed more hard liquor
Than what he'd hid beneath his sack.
He barged aboard a tied-up steamer
And found a case of gin, some creamer,
A loaf of cheese — that was enough:
John grabbed the gin and other stuff —
As much as his poor arms could mule —
And would have left the ship, but that
Was not his fate; instead a rat
Appeared and challenged him to duel,
Produced a tiny pistol, fired:
John Back lay dead, wiped out, expired.

Sk8

To hurl—on wheels and board—oneself upon
A curving plane that uses gravity
To bring a blending of geometry and bone

Is one way to describe the breaking dawn
Of simple unexpected sanity
That turns the wheels and board one's self's upon

When dropping in and tuning out the spawn
Of shallow crowded life's cacophony
To bring a bending of geometry and bone

Pythagorean-like when now it hits the brain
Reflecting back from later history
To hurl the wheels and boards these thoughts are on,

To wonder at one's youth and scattered train
Of visions climbing caves of memory,
To blink at blinding light's geometry and bone,

To light the heavens up, undone, alone,
For one sweet moment's flagrant mystery,
To hurl—on wheels and board—oneself upon
The burning blending of geometry and bone.

The Bed

That Sunday morning we arose from love,
In love, with love, of love, from the bed
We shared, that lovely bed we'd made from dreams,
That sweet bed that held us as I held you
As you held me, that bed, that bed, that bed.
Our love transformed that humble bed into
The bed of beds, our love unhinged that bed
And sent it floating, flying, bending, wed
To all the love the world has ever known,
To all the joy two bodies can contain.
We rose up from our bed, our happy bed,
And found our way downstairs to breakfast,
Our love transforming every sip of coffee,
Every bite of melon, every taste
And touch and sight and smell and every sound.

The One I Love

The one I love is wisped with wind, the air
Around her skin spins and eddies there
Creating weather in her eyes, her hair.

The one I love is like the country sky,
Open wide and calm, recalling why
The world is good but gone and gone awry.

The one I love remembers me in all
She does, in every thought, in every call
For help when I am there to catch her fall.

The one I love is in my mind, my arms,
When I find space to occupy her charms
And she finds time to wake to my alarms.

The one I love is in my arms, my bed,
Sleeping, waking, waiting to be wed.

If I Could Fly

If I could fly
My plane to you
I'd put the sky
Into my shoe
And make my way
Across the blue
In half a day
That's what I'd do

To spend the evening
Touching you
And then the morning
Through and through
And on and on
And deep into
Your dusk my dawn
Our one from two

Rubaiyat on a Summer Day

We went to the bus stop, my daughters and I,
But the bus didn't come — we just looked at the sky.
We missed the damn bus, but that was okay,
We walked into Starbucks and drank — we were dry.

Then we hustled back out in the heat of the day
To catch the next bus that was headed our way.
We paid the buck-fifty, selected our seats,
Sat back and enjoyed the roll and the sway.

We got off at the Plaza, where everyone meets,
And marveled at big cats, skywalked across streets.
Soon we were down where the river flows by,
Searching for crawdads, blackberries, and treats.

Poetry Is Not Dead

This just in: Poetry is not dead.
Anemic namby-pamby bambies
tied it in double-knotted bows
and clicked shut the coffin lid on it.
Acrid academicians marinated it in formaldehyde
and sealed it in jars with pig latin labels.
The county medical examiner pronounced it
dead
and rolled an extra large recycled plastic simulated rock
across the hole.
The general public glanced
at the obituary in the Sunday paper
before moving on to the ads for all the
the Chamber of Commerce endorsed, utter crap proposed
to fill the chasm of everydayness
that is the world without poetry.

They thought poetry was dead,
but like skateboarding and sex and the glory of the Lord
it's back
and everyone is doing it
for the sheer fucking fun of it.
Everyone's putting pen to paper
to conjure the ghosts of the present tense,
to forge in the smithy of their souls
the stand-up tragicomedy of the silent chaos
that surrounds us.

There is no need to hide, no need
to deride the people who have seen
a great light, who have stood together
under a streetlight to spite the night,
who have unrolled the manufactured boulder of apathy
away from the electronic tomb of despondent distraction
and found there is a there there —
and it flows with dollar beer and grilled
cheese sandwiches and love.

I am the resurrection
sayeth the Lord
and the life and I AM
poetry
and I live.
I am da way and da truth, yo, and I
am I and I
am poetry, bitch, and I live in you and you in me,
so hand me that beer, brother,
and step up to the mic.
Quite the contrary it is not dead,
it was only sleeping,
nursing a hangover
after a Keatsian bender.
But hare of the dog, it liveth!
So flip that switch, sister,
and put your mouth up to the microphone,
dial it in,
because poetry is no sin
and poetry is not
no is not
dead.

Que tous vos désirs se réalisent

The bells and flowers ringing in my ears
Tell me your birthday came again this year
With snowy birds and flaming ribbons,
With footnote revelries packaged for remembrance.
The apples of your eyes reminded me
That gravity holds us both to the patient Earth
And that it won't be long before the tulips
And daffodils, red and yellow, break through
To outer space, colliding like atoms and breaking
Into the shimmering constancy of your eyes
Looking into mine—and mine finding
The candles of your every cake, your every
Secret wish—wished anew—come true.

Outside the Campus Dental Clinic

For some reason I was standing there,
Behind this older female faculty chair,
And watched her pluck a strand of hair.
It was with such casual intent
That thumb and forefinger went
Right to where they were meant,
But it took her another try or two
To find the perfect one, to do
What she intended to,
Which was to use it (it was no loss)
For dental floss.

My Mother Urs

My mother Urs
Is not averse
To what is claimed
To be not worse

Like apple cores
And wooden floors
And husbands blamed
For broken doors

But woe betide
The other side
If they, enflamed
Should try her pride

For she will cut
Their fattened butt
Unfurl her famed
Derisive tut

And bring them low
To eat some crow
Till they be lamed
And in the know

My Father Ted

My father Ted
Can take the lead
From bullets aimed
Straight at his head

And turn them in
To gold and tin
To cure the maimed
Both friend and kin

By alchemy
And family tree
And things unnamed
And mystery

Because he knows
The wild rose
Cannot be tamed
It only grows

With rooted love
And hand and glove
And old age framed
By the sky above

My Sister Jean

My sister Jean
Is in between
The age of reason
And the guillotine

The rock of ages
And Elizabeth's stages
The ring of fire
And my back pages

She's getting older
And getting bolder
About the contents
Of her secret folder

She's got some news
To heal your blues
So listen up
Take off your shoes

Have a slice
Of cake that's nice
And say happy birthday
But don't say it twice

My Daughter Holl

My daughter Holl
Will rise and fall
With music notes
That pitch and stall

She'll bend the facts
In second acts
And sing the words
That truth extracts

She'll paint and draw
Outside the law
To make a place
For beauty's flaw

And bend the light
Into a flight
Of colored stairs
That leave her sight

And then she'll turn
Her face to yearn
For summer in
November's burn

My Daughter Dyl

My daughter Dyl
Is strong of will
And will persist
Right up the hill

To win the prize
That's in her eyes
To help a friend
Who fell to rise

She has a vision
A firm decision
To make things better
Through light revision

And when she laughs
There are giraffes
Who topple into
Music staffs

But when she's tough
And feeling gruff
Then there are zebras
Who huff and puff

My Daughter at Seven

When you were in the womb the
World was a perilous place.
The doctors were full of doubts
About you staying where you
Were, where you needed to be
To do the work of being
And becoming a person.

But you stubbornly stayed put,
Your mother remained calm, your
Sister and I observed the
Hours until you arrived—
A shock of black hair on your
Head, contentment on your face,
Dreams brewing in your dark eyes.

Summer was upon us and
The perils of the world turned
Soft as butter. Your sister
Looked after you with us and
Soon you were smiling, walking,
Talking, singing, doing all
That young and thriving souls will.

You loved baby dolls and soon
You had a few with cribs and
Cradles spread around your room
For lullabies and naptimes.
Hand-me-down princess dresses
From your sister turned the world
Into a magical place.

And when we went to Disney-
Land, you wore a different dress
Each day and demanded that
I fly you from ride to ride,
Which I was glad to do as
Best I could, to simulate
The proper mode of travel.

For you were light as feathers
And I was a gust of wind
Thrilled to lift you up and take
You places. You went to school,
Following your sister's paths,
But carving your own unique
Grooves and stylings on the way.

Now you're seven and it's been
A breakthrough year — up, down,
Spinning all around — breakthrough!
Swimming, soccer, monkey bars,
Learning to ride a bike all
On your own. Ukulele!
Roller skates! How I love you.

My Daughter at Ten

My daughter was born at the edge of day
When autumn's equinox was a distant
Memory, the days in our northern town
Narrowing down like light through a keyhole,
Her mother and I praying for that light
To shine in our dawning daughter's heart that
First day, praying for wisdom to show her —
You — the way to open the door and let
The light flood in to fill the room of her
Life with the light there waiting in her eyes.

We brought you home, uncertain of how to
Love you with the love that overwhelmed us,
How to protect you from our own mistakes
And the mistakes of others everywhere
That swirl round Earth's atmosphere unaware
Of fragile just-born beings lying there,
Asleep, soft, smelling of springtime dewdrops,
Moon petals, sunbeam sweet pea barley tea,
How to keep you safe from danger but not
Safe from love, not safe from every good thing.

Some time passed, the sun and the moon sped by,
Birds flew, dogs barked in their turn, words upon
Words piled up all around you, wooden blocks
Formed into towers to tumble, we moved
To a new house, bigger, with a big yard,
Grandparents kept watch in their turn, new friends
Appeared, new places were tried, names turned over
On lips and tongue with laughter and cries of
Joy and dismay, aunts, uncles, and cousins,
Walks in the park, everything happening.

You were as precocious as the sunrise,
Singing and speaking, running and walking,

In and out of everything, your mind a
Light, your eyes open, your heart burning flames
Made of music and color, and yes, you
Gave us some trouble, too, we not always
Able to contain the spilling over
Urgency of wonder you couldn't stop,
And then your sister was born and you were
The guide to her light, the sister teacher.

Preschool, Kindergarten, teachers smiling
Into your light, letting their warmth and yours
Merge in moments of time, good friends and best
Friends concocting adventures on the spot,
Scooters, skinned knees, nature walks, collecting
Pinecones, leaves, bugs, rocks, slugs, crawdads, fairies,
You learned by going, learned to ride a bike,
First on a grassy slope, then on a broad
Expanse of flat asphalt near an ice cream
Shop, and finally on sidewalks and streets.

You paved the world in reams of paper drawn
With pen and ink, pencil and paint, light and dark
Imagined things drawn from the world and made
New by the newness of you, you sang songs
Made out of the same intricate dreamstuff
And carried on dramatic productions,
Star-crossed narratives, comedic word play,
And I looked at you and your sister in
The rearview mirror, wondering at all
The mystery let loose within your souls.

The uniform you wore you wore so well
Back then, not for uniformity's sake
But for the sake of style and tradition,
For the way the light shown on the fabric,
The way a kind of music played across
The pattern, especially when you sang

In the bleak midwinter, poor as I am,
What can I give him, give to him my heart,
When you sang that in the Cathedral with
All of heaven's angels pausing to hear.

Earth stood hard as iron then, but summer
Softened the world and warmed the changing time
With a view of the strong flowing river
Where it came down from the falls past children
Playing, you and your new and old friends there,
And then a new school, new teachers, new light
On old thoughts growing and changing, looking
Past the past to see continuity
In all things, past the future to see the
Present moment resting there in your heart.

That moment of rest is there inside you
Always and forever for you to hold
Steady when you need to and you will find
A river of light flows through in full and
Bursting life and love, love of mother, love
Of father, sister, grandparents, cousins,
Aunts and uncles, friends and teachers, angels,
Saints, and God the source and fountain of love,
The love that there is no hiding from, the
Love that will never ever leave your side.

I am writing this on the eve of your
Tenth birthday and I cannot find the words
To say how much you mean to me, Holland,
To say how I am still as overwhelmed
As the day you were born, still overwhelmed
With love for you, still blinking in the light
Of you, still drinking in the mystery
And the majesty of you, and praying
For the wisdom to know how to let you
Open your door and fill the world with light.

Epithalamium

Your dad could strum a chord for the groom's ironic
Soul, pluck notes for the bride's unbridled heart.
The river could rush inevitably down the cataracts,
With music of mountains and trees and love and hurt.
Quotidian mysteries could rise like bread in ovens
With alphabetic fingertips at work
Assaying life and life's atomic leavens
Filamented against the blooming dark.
And pouring off of certain pages of the local
Paper could come the haunted words of unbound
Laughter smashing through the wall to tickle
Tattooed limbs with the music of the mind.
What could be is on the verge: the wedding knot
Is tied to the bridge and the strings are strung tonight.

Your dad's guitar could play from heaven a psalm
Of David connecting stretched, refashioned strings
And bent blues turned into bliss's home,
The hallelujah wrung from righted wrongs.
The sky could cry, the ground could disappear
Beneath your feet, only to expand in daylight
Revealing oceanic paths of freer
Joys than you imagined in the gnarled night.
And schooled physicians with their evidence of cures
Could wrestle with your intellects and find
Themselves at odds with your inner music's tears
Turned into a gladness they can't understand.
Undo the funeral dirge; the wedding knot
Is tied to the bridge and the strings are tuned tonight.

Your father played a song when you were in
The womb, with river running to the rhythm
Of ingrained momentum's long and winding
Road that led to this day's bridged chasm.
The tuning fork in the road reversed to blend

The bramble and rumble of muscled motor city
With virginal violins and warbling stands
Of Douglas fir—gritty and pretty in harmony.
And parsed-entangled visions of the future
Stretch across the threshold of the room
Where the end of May is perched on June's shoulder,
And blessings shower down with tears from him.
Two melodies now merge—the wedding knot
Is tied to the bridge and the strings are strummed tonight.

Every Child's Place

Above the trees the sky is bright:
The sunny day, the starry night.
Around the world the children play,
Their minds are bright both night and day.
Sometimes we dream, sometimes we sing,
We each have gifts that we can bring.
Our hearts fill up with love and peace,
Breathe in, breathe out, let love increase.
This place is ours, our roots grow deep,
Our arms reach out to give and keep.
Sometimes we bend, sometimes we fall,
But helping hands help us stand tall.
And we in turn will help our friends —
The circle turns, it never ends.

Confirmation

A Webb named Thomas went to church
To get confirmed and find a perch
Whereon to land when in the lurch.

His sister Honor went there too
To find the truth that's truly true
And follow mystery's grand clue.

These twins arrived and stood before
The steps that led up to the door;
And up they went, it was no chore.

The priest said: You two were baptized
Because in Christ your souls were prized,
And now you're here, God's not surprised.

So say a prayer of the thanks and joy
And board the ship—ahoy, ahoy!

Otto Zehm in Heaven

... he always came to work with a two-liter of Pepsi and a gallon of milk. He said it kept his hair shining and flowing. —The Inlander

He wears a crown and plays guitar and hands
out Snickers bars to anyone who looks
like they might like one.
They didn't have
Snickers bars in heaven
when Otto arrived,
but now they do.
They didn't have Pepsi, either,
and they still don't.
Otto said that wouldn't be necessary.
But they do have milk,
by the gallon,
and the gallant cows they get it from
moo and murmur in harmony
when Otto plays his guitar,
they moo like angels might
if angels could be cows,
they moo like Eddie Van Halen's guitar would moo
if it were made of magic cowhide,
they moo and wail and their mooing
and wailing shake the mountains of heaven
when Otto plays the guitar,
the guitar that Jesus gave him
on the third day,
the day he was released from his chains.

When Otto looks through the mists of heaven
down into the realms of earth,
he sees his mother and smiles.
And he sees the turmoil,
the fretting and stealing,
the anxious knuckles, the discolored teeth,
the paychecks and the ATMs,
the St. Patrick's Day parades
with officers in polished uniforms.
He sees the souls of his friends
and the soul of a girl named Amber,
the confused and clamoring
souls of our city, the city of man.
And he sees the dark soul
of the man who murdered him,
brooding in a garden in a back yard.
The man waits on the word *prison*
and eyes the spindle of obstructed justice.
Otto sees this man,
sees him clearly sometimes,
and his radiant soul is moved
with pity. His guitar cries out to this man
and the cows of heaven moo and give their milk.

Walla Walla Bike Ride

One of the joys here is to ride out
From under the trees and housetops,
Out and up to the open pastures and wheat fields
Deep, rich, thick, brown, and green,
Of dirt and grass. All the distances,
Groomed by strong good hands, stretching
Out to hills of same but far away translucent colors.
And you breathe, and you realize that you
Haven't breathed for a long time
And that one doesn't really breathe
Beneath the trees and housetops.
You might ride out on Park Street, for example.
Busy people will be driving home
Or to work in town where you begin.
You cross Stone Creek, Tietan Park,
A schoolyard on the left, a graveyard on the right,
Then pastures and fields and horses
And the smell of horses and other creatures
And their smells, deep rich smells
And deep rich colors, and the same colors
Translucent in the distant hills, softening, fading.
You now cross over a real country creek
And you press on up a gradual hill
And you smell your own sweat.
And your own thighs like horses' thighs
Tighten, and the air is cool and your ears
Are a little cold, you notice as the land
Flattens out and extends and widens.
And your soul breathes as far as your eyes see.
Then you come to a place where the road forks
And you stop. One way leads straight out
Toward the hills to the left, and the other curves
To the right perhaps back to another part of the town,
To more trees and housetops.
You pause and think how way leads on

To way. But the graveyard you passed
On the outskirts of town calls you back
The same way you came. You turn around
And glide down toward town, past horses
And dogs and cows and young calves.
All that you saw before, you are now glad to see
Again, and you are still breathing
All the distances you have seen
Because you remember.
And you name the animals as you pass them.
Then you come to the graveyard,
Which is itself bordered by a farm and a field.
You can sneak into the graveyard, in fact,
At the corner of this farm because
There is no fence. Fence posts, but no fence.
You walk your bike now, past insistent tulip leaves
Just broken through the debris of fall,
Down the path that is separated from the road
By an old white wooden fence on your right.
On your left are gravestones, and you read
The names. Some names you have never heard.
There is an old man riding his bike,
He wears an orange hat, his big dog runs freely
Across the grass. You turn in toward the heart
Of the cemetery. You look up at looming trees
With limbs not yet leaved. You read more names
And dates. Some have only birth dates—
Widows waiting to depart this shore.
You can imagine them living in town somewhere,
The old ladies one meets in church.
There are various styles of gravestones,
Some obscured by sediment and brown leaves.
Should you brush this off? you think
Of one gravestone. You realize you should not.
You think you would like perhaps to be buried here
And have a small flat gravestone.
The upright gravestones look fragile.

You pass the man in the orange hat.
Now the dog is on a rope and is pulling the man
Along on his bike. They are leaving.
You come to the rows of white where soldiers lie.
The wind begins to blow a little harder,
The flag flies, which is always at half mast,
The sun is setting beyond. You walk toward it,
Your shadow lengthening out behind you.
You come to the main road that leads out
Of the cemetery. You get on your bike and ride,
Your shadow lengthening out beside you.

This was the journey
I just returned from, and it all seemed
Very much like a dream.

I Will Stay Beside You

Let me not admit November's wild
Transition into winter's dark, my child,
Could ever turn the light out in your mind
Or cause the love within you to unbind.
Oh no, you woke in autumn's grip but kept
It at arm's length until you walked and leapt
Across the calendar of time and thought
And showed me everything you found and brought
From icy mornings to the changing seasons,
From cold conclusions to the warming reasons,
To daughter me to father forth my vision,
To light a fire of love and firm decision,
To love you always, always newly prove
That I will stay beside you, never move.

Beyond Compare

What shall I compare thee to, my child?
A gentle breeze in June at times gone wild,
A bird that perches in my soul and sings
And then takes flight on wise and beautiful wings,
A leaf that shimmers in the early light of June,
A branch, a tree, a ukulele tune,
A happy thought, a perfect plan, a hand
That reaches out to help and understand,
A string on my guitar that plays a note
That no one could have guessed, an antidote
To things exactly as they are — to winter —
A keen-eyed tweezer pulling out a splinter.
My daughter, you are you beyond compare —
I'm glad to simply breathe your lovely air.

Thirty Years

Thirty years
Ago it was
Shifting gears
Above the buzz
Of broken grief
Of lost pain
A brand-new leaf
We can't explain
Branches grafted
Mended limbs
Revisions drafted
Of old hymns
That sing between
Mike and Jean

Valentine's

On Valentine's
I'd like to say
I see the signs
And hear the neigh-
Ing of apoc-
Alyptic horses
And the tock
And tick of courses
Flooding down
From broken dams
Upon my town,
Its goats and lambs,
To drown us all
In Love's thrall

Valentine for Dylan

My daughter Dyllie
This valentine
's not willy-nilly
It is my sign
My deepest smile
And joyful tear
From every mile
We've traveled here
In lovely time
Under the blue
To find the rhyme
Of me and you
So happy day
My love will stay

Valentine for Holland

My daughter Holly
This valentine
Is like a trolley
On the line
From me to you
Electrified
And rolling true
From far and wide
To say a word
To give a message
A little bird
A secret passage
Right above you
To say I love you

Valentine for Natalie

Mon amour
St. Valentine
Opened the door
And let us in
To be alive
With love and skin
Not just survive
But drink the wine
Of you and me
And eat the bread
Of mystery
And so to bed
To make such love
The angels gather up above

Valentine for Myself

I wrote
My name
A note
Of fame
With pen
And ink
I ken
And think
I can
Explain
A plan
So sane
Imbibe
To scribe

Ursie Marie

Ursie Marie
Looked to the skies
Above a tree
That never dies.
God looked down
And saw her there,
A verb-like noun
With adjective hair.
"Greetings, Urs,"
God said with a smile,
"There is no curse
Down the road a mile."
Ursula nodded
And the tree applauded.

Theodore Lee

Theodore Lee
At four score
Entered his plea
At God's door.
God said, "Ted,
The jig's not up,
Time has sped
To fill your cup
And now you've got
Time to drink,
Thicken the plot,
And spill some ink;
So take a swig
And dance that jig."

TAC

Todd Ardell Curtis,
you were an enigma from
beginning to end.

The places in you
that beckoned to your angels
bedeviled you, too.

Was it money that
caused reality to fall
flat across your path?

And was it disease
that caused those flare-ups in you
that strained at the seams

of what seems and is
the love and friendship sorely
found and lost and saved?

You pursued some dream
that eluded you even
as you held it close.

Did I love you? Yes.
But not enough, I confess,
to open my eyes.

Year in Review

Dear friends the Earth is spinning wildly
While stars collide and comets zing.
The universe, to put it mildly,
Is fucking strange and has a sting.
The beast of Bethlehem is breathing
In our breath, and time is seething
To feel it swirling down the drain,
Derailing like a wayward train.
O Death, your lipstick and mascara
And holiday cards at Christmastime
Can't hide from us your latest crime —
We see your camera obscura.
O Death, dear friends, let us recall
The painful light that woke us all.

The Pillows

the pillows of night
turn over to the cool side
spring wakes up summer

Your Birthday in Montreal

As 2018 comes to an end

The melted snow that turned to sheets of ice
For us to slide across and roll like dice
Or glide on blades and once or twice to slice
Our skin or to begin to say that's nice
Let's warm our bones with spicy curry, rice,
And witty reportage regarding mice
And other creatures forced to pay the price —
When suddenly the year wound down to end,
Your birthday came and I was there to bend
To every wish your diagram might wend
Into its circles overlapping, penned
By Venn for pigs and elephants to tend,
Our love exploding *or* and *not* and *and*
Beyond what Boolean nerds can comprehend.

Sonnets from London

1.

My dear my first and hard to fathom daughter
Undangling from the sky to land on earth
From when the stars had names and injured birds
Began to weep their wings retracted in
And pain within a fist your pulse unchecked
The universe sprawled out beneath your feet
Because perhaps a god required it to.
That's how the hammer drove the nail right through
The wood and right into your lovely sweet
Persistent thoughts of all the wrecker wrecked
The pull of tightness deep beneath your skin
And pain a rope from broken thoughts to words
From swinging anchors ballerinas birth
To grappling hooks thrown from your teeter totter

2.

My darling daughter second one to come
Along a miracle at midnight's music
Simplicity unsimple majesty's
Humility in deeply unafraid
And sympathetic whimsy-worn approaches
For others and for you for every thing
Beneath the blessed sun around the bend.
You didn't have to try to comprehend
The meaning of the song you had to sing
From lungs and laughing lips and frowns of coaches
In consequential games and beds unmade
And made to work and then to take your ease
On trampolines of comic-tragic panic
While love beats to your heart's eternal drum

3.

Love of my London tired-legged life
From Holland Park to Piccadilly Line
I follow you and take the lead and walk
Beside you up and down and thither yon
Beyond into upon the journey through
And through and through the rain the sun the sense
And sensibility with dedication.
The burdens of our lengthiest vacation
The curse of Scotland black cat recompense
For unnamed unforgotten dreams untrue
Beneath our love we're both of us long gone
And sitting at a table filled with talk
My pencil sharpened to a point too fine
To capture you as my unbridled wife

4.

You taller than I would have thought a missing
Recovered puzzle piece of puzzled love
Sub-basement friendship in the brink of time
Pretending to be shielded by a shell
Of sternly humoured alter-ego blades
Not knives of grass that gently touch the air
And reach the mind not minding what's in store.
I mark my words and shepherd them to shore
On clippers under bridges to declare
The accents spent the syntax and parades
Protruding through the stillness of the spell
That London casts against its tidy grime
Reflected in your clever push and shove
And to the music of the teapots hissing

5.

The man to man connected by a bond
Requited and ignited in the mind
Without impediments from Liverpool
To London on reconnaissance's will
A stalwart steady soul and full of gazing
A psalmist's name an amiability
Like Jonathan's it could be truly said.
To London you arrived and soon you fled
To Copenhagen then to VBC
To illustrate that two by two appraising
This life can be progressively uphill
To overlooks that teach the golden rule
Sequential strategies of love aren't blind
Expecting expectation's great beyond

6.

I hold your London hand in mine and kiss
Your London lips the Thames could overflow
And wash our bed down to the flagrant sea
Down to the stormy sea but quietly
But quietly my love breathe carefully
And we will sleep perchance to dream of sleep
But first I kiss your London lips again.
You are the girl I'm dreaming of within
My dream of dreaming as I climb the steep
The spiral stair to seek you prayerfully
Uncomprehend the end to make your plea
For morning and the sun poetically
Arisen from what's going on below
When I can hold your London hand in bliss

7.

Museum-weary days of introspective
Meandering among the captured fogs
Of things half brought to life on London's streets
With mischief-making prodding poking mum
And jostling joshing squeezing testing patience
While she endures imagination's call
Maintained by energetic walking round.
Your second time in London would astound
The boy from Montreal whose basketball
Was laid aside to broaden adolescence
In London's brisk and buoyant cheery hum
Along the Thames and underground retreats
From station mind the gap to puddle slogs
Vacation's educational corrective

8.

Behind the double decker bus of pain
Above the underground belief in motion
Within walled gardens of the blooms' delight
There may be clues that lead to 40B
Near Paddington Station and Little Venice's
Canals grown derelict in elegance
Where I would like to travel in my dreams.
When science falters at its many schemes
The days grow weary where they pitch their tents
The night falls from what daily darkness does
Then I would like to be and not to be
While sitting in the brightness of your bright
Unvanishing and pleasant resting notion
Of eating chips and drinking bright champagne

9.

So what's to be my love my love to be
When all that I can do is lovingly
Surrender to the ravages of ego
And sensitivity's museum of
The soul's beleaguered blunted dread of smallness
Picasso's trio in the modern Tate
That started realistic but got turned.
Your face will face me and your eyes not spurned
Will look into me as I rise up late
To tell you without words you are my allness
In moments meeting on the fringe of love
While worlds go spinning by and we go
For cappuccino foam so longingly
A delicate and foreign bird set free

10.

The waters flow the paterfamilias
Bestows on us a pouring out of clout
To bring us through the sky and set us here
With sunrise eggs and toast delivered with
Incisive comments cheerily conveyed
And commonsense appraisals of the doings
Of fools and statesmen, friends and foes and wives.
The journey thus laid out to open lives
Begins like clever brewers brew their brewings
To percolate the magistrates' parade
And bring about a questioning of myth
Combined with bottles large of Cobra beer
Cracked open at the table of our doubt
To bind and challenge and to humour us

11.

In nicks of time the times do nick and pluck
The strings and stroke the canvases with colour
Impressionistically Trafalgar Square
Unfurls its bienvenue lions géants
To usher you into the galleries
Both national and otherwise to see
And feel with other sense Monsieur Renoir.
Your eyes with spectacles inspect the au revoir
Of 1800s' out of focus glee
For gorgeous smears and sensibilities
Umbrellas flowers round-faced girls on loan
From France to London in the foul and fair
Of days that alternate from bright to duller
While you consider bad and better luck

12.

The peacocks parakeets and waterfowl
Of London statues here and there well-placed
The mud occasional the sun's instructions
To look to left to see your face to smile
To arm and arm against the wind to find
The route that suits us best by tube by bus
By walking vigorous and pleasant paths.
Beneath our feet the ruins of some baths
Leftover from the Roman times for us
To ponder as we wend our way aligned
With one another's mile for mile for mile
Mapped out by pigeons and unkind obstructions
From dogs whose owners seem to have some haste
Back to our room's bidet and heated towel

13.

Fidelio fiddles with the interval
Between Acts One and Two as I sneak in
Behind advice and worried glances from
The seats in front of where I take my stand
Defending scoundrel moves I make in life
Within my mind while Florestan may have
Contracted something to obscure his voice.
I glance down at your hair affirms my choice
Applying to my conscience love the salve
With no regret the opera house is rife
With plans arising from what is unplanned
Like fingers finding novel notes to strum
Martinis made from vodka or from gin
And thoughts of you I muse upon and mull

14.

Tomorrow and tomorrow seemed so far
From yesterday's reality when we
Arrived with visions of the Globe and plans
For day by day excursions hand in hand
A year has passed I send my SOS
To you my message in the bottle
To dance me to the end of love my love.
From Montreal Spokane convergence of
Your life and mine in London dawdle
We both of us surrender more from less
As days undwindle down to what's unplanned
Devotion to deny the travel bans
That keep us trapped upon the stormy sea
But we will be together and we are

The Air / Your Hair

The air	Your hair
Expands	My hands
Desire	On fire
For funds	The hounds
To come	A drum
To you	Your shoe
Your dream	Does seem
Your eye	To sigh
Make truth	Sweet tooth
Make Love	Above
Your teeth	Beneath
I crave	This wave
To reach	Will teach
To touch	Us much

October Evening

It is October.
I'm outside at 8:30
Having built a fire

I drank some whiskey
There are wispy clouds above
And a noisy plane

My dog is here too
I hear his collar jingle
as he roams the yard

He likes being out
Here with me in the evening
Sniffing the fall air

I am reciting these
Lines of haiku syllables
Into my smartphone

The fire burns low
Occasionally crackles
My mind also roams

The yard of my life
My past experiences
Sniffing for a clue

Manito

There is a tree in the park
That stands on its own like a
Salvaged reminder of pain,
A souvenir of the time
We all went through something dark
And survived to take the sun.
I visit that tree often
And take in its damaged form
Now grown into beautiful
Breath breathing upwards to sky,
Like looking in a mirror
At my own soul arising.

Self-Portrait with Wife

we stand together
before the stark shimmering
gliding mirrored doors

our bedroom closet
lurks behind, the hardwood floor
beneath our feet, mine

bare, yours with black socks,
our bed of bliss stretched out there
behind us, covered

by a flower print
comforter that's sometimes thrown
aside in hot fits,

the laundry basket
empty and waiting for the
next load of colors,

my arm wrapped round you
with my wristwatch on fingers
clutching your shoulder,

your nose obscured by
a smudge where skin perhaps has
nuzzled the mirror,

the dresser, the lamp,
your son's painting, the winter
scene, the jewelry box,

the almost hidden
books, and, over to the side,
my socks black like yours

Becoming Myself

becoming myself
could actually happen
i believe it could

on a rainy day
as leaves fall and paste themselves
to pavements and feet

walking familiar
paths to places known too well
shod in shoes worn out

if i were a rich man
counting money like syllables
then maybe i could rest

in increasing luxury
like a poem forming line by line
instead of worrying time

but i am more like
a haiku stanza falling
into line with you

and wishing i could
become myself with vengeance
and take you with me

123

Epilogue

Elsie on the Farm

The harvest gathered in, you sat and played
A piece that gathered years within its frame.

You watched your memories like a parade
File by you to the music that you made.

But when you finished, time had seemed to blame
The present for its lonesome fruitfulness.

Your children and grandchildren went and came
In patterns of the new and age-old game.

You stepped outside and felt the air caress
Your forehead like a kiss from long ago.

The moon was low, and something seemed to bless
The ground you stood on with a loveliness

Anticipating winter's covering snow
And bulbs down deep calmly waiting to grow.

Acknowledgements

"Tulips for Elsie" and "Seventy Syllables for My Mother" appear in *Dappled Things*

"The Condom" appears in *RiverLit*

"Audubon's Lament" and "When I Was Broke" appear in *San Diego Reader*

"Rubaiyat on a Summer Day" appears in *Railtown Almanac*

"Manito" appears in *In the Neighborhood*

"Tom I. Davis" appears in *Spokane Writes*

"Mark Anderson" and "The Night Before the First Day of School" appear in *Pictures of Poets*

"Short Story" was presented at *Verbatim*

"Sk8" was presented at *Only Time Will Tell*

"Driving Down Division" was presented at *Hotel Spokane*

"The River" was presented at *The 50-Hour Slam*

"Tulips for Elsie," "When I Was Broke," "I Want You," "Stopping by Blogs on a Frosty Evening," "Sk8," "The Bed," "If I Could Fly," "Every Child's Place," "Valentine for Natalie," "Self-Portrait with Wife," and Sonnet from London #6 appear on *The Writer's Almanac*

Sources Referenced

Agzigian, Z. 2008. *Stamen and whirlwind*, Spokane, Wash.: Gribble Press.

Alexie, S., 1996. *The summer of black widows*, Brooklyn, N.Y.: Hanging Loose Press.

Anderson, M., 2020. A cross generational collaboration poem — the crown leaves scattered, Spokane, Wash.: TEDxSpokane.

Austin, C.W. & Scott, H. S, 1966. *The great Seattle fire of June 6th, 1889: containing a succinct and complete account of the greatest conflagration on the Pacific coast*, Seattle, Wash.: Shorey.

Beethoven, L.van et al., 1851. *Fidelio: an opera in two acts*, London: T. Brettell.

Campbell, H., 1966. *All good families are alike*, Santa Barbara, Calif.: Mesa School Lane Books.

Caraway, T.E., 2007. *What the sky lacks*, Spokane, Wash.: Korrektiv Press.

Cohen, L., 1988. *I'm your man*, New York: Columbia.

Cummings, E.E., 1923. *Tulips and chimneys*, New York: T. Seltzer.

Davis, T.I., 2000. *The Little Spokane*, Spokane, Wash.: Lost Horse Press.

Deshais, N. Oct 12, 2011. Otto Zehm, Spokane, Wash.: *The Inlander*.

Dylan, B., 2003. *Blonde on blonde*, New York: Columbia.

Frost, R., 1923. *New Hampshire*, New York: Henry Holt and Company.

Held, D., 2001. *Betting on the night*, Sandpoint, Idaho: Lost Horse Press.

Howell, C., 1977. *The crime of luck*, Sunderland, Mass.: Panache Books.

Johnson, J., 2001. *Mastodon, 80% complete*, Pittsburgh, Penn.: Carnegie Mellon University Press.

Olson, K. 2014. *National poetry slam finals showcase*, Oakland, Calif.: Poetry Slam, Inc.

Percy, W. 1961. *The moviegoer*, New York, N.Y.: Knopf.

Pushkin, A. 1833. *Eugene Onegin*, St. Petersburg: Znanie.

Red Hot Chili Peppers. 2011. *I'm with you*, Beverly Hills, Calif.: Warner Reprise Maverick.

Shakespeare, W., 1609. Shake-speares sonnets neuer before imprinted, London: G. Eld for TT, solde by William Aspley.

Simon, P. 1986. *Graceland*, Los Angeles, Calif.: Warner Bros.

Toor, R., 2008. *Personal record: a love affair with running*, Lincoln, Neb.: University of Nebraska Press.

Walter, J., 2001. *Over tumbled graves*, New York: Regan Books.

Wright, C., 2017. *This dream the world: new and selected poems*, Sandpoint, Idaho: Lost Horse Press.

About the Author

Photo by Natalie Waters

Jonathan Potter is a skater, a librarian, and the author of *House of Words* (Korrektiv Press, 2010). His poetry also appears in the *Imago Dei, Railtown Almanac*, and *Spokane Writes* anthologies, in a variety of journals, and on *The Writer's Almanac* radio show and podcast. At various times and places from 2010 to 2020, Potter hosted *Naked Lunch Break* (a lunchtime poetry open mic and reading series), moderated the *Poets of the Pacific Northwest* and *Poetry Salon* panels at the Get Lit! literary festival, and contributed work to the *Hotel Spokane, Only Time Will Tell, Verbatim, Pictures of Poets,* and *The 50-Hour Slam* poet/artist/photographer/filmmaker collaborative projects, happenings, and exhibits. He lives and works in Spokane, Washington, and can sometimes be found in Montreal.

A Note on the Type

The text of this book is set in Cochin,
a typeface originally produced in 1912
by Georges Peignot for the Paris foundry,
G. Peignot et Fils (later Deberny & Peignot),
and was based on the copperplate engravings of
18th-century French artist
Charles-Nicolas Cochin.

Made in the USA
Columbia, SC
15 May 2021